Getting to Joy

A MOTHER'S JOURNEY OF INFERTILITY, MISCARRIAGE, AND STILLBIRTH

TACOLE ROBINSON

EDITED BY
NICOLE QUEEN

VISION PUBLISHING
HOUSE

To all of the parents who long to hold their child in their arms, but instead are forced to hold them in their hearts...

In honor of Deja Joy...

My pursuit of you led me on a journey to pure *joy*.
I am better because of you.
Mama loves you!

Contents

Scan below
to listen to the
Introduction
read by the
author.

Introduction

Introduction

I am *happy glad* that you have chosen to go on this journey with me. Please continue to read this introduction. Do not skip over it like I often do! I promise you the organization of the book will make more sense if you just give me a few moments.

So if you are a person who pays attention to details, you may be wondering a few things. Why are there bubbles? What's up with the butterflies? Why is the title on a dirt path?

Let's start with the title *Getting to JOY*. The concept for this book developed through my struggle with conceiving and giving birth. I knew I was supposed to be a mother biologically. I knew that I knew that I knew. No one could tell me otherwise. Not my husband. Not my family. Not the doctors.

I had a dream about this beautiful brown-skinned little girl. She had two beautiful afro puffs, and we were sitting in my grandmother's living room. The dream was like déjà vu. From that moment on, I named her Deja Joy, and I looked forward to meeting her on earth.

My husband and I eventually conceived fourteen years later and were elated to find out we were pregnant with our little girl. This pregnancy was not like the previous one. It was without issues with high blood pressure. There was such a peace and joy. I spent many days of the pregnancy blowing bubbles with my children as we awaited Deja Joy's arrival. Thus, the incorporation of bubbles in this book.

I initially thought this book was about getting to Deja Joy. I later discovered God wants me to share my journey of getting to JOY. Becoming a mother came with real challenges and many disappointments. I found light in the midst of darkness. I experienced comfort in the midst of pain. Thus, the incorporation of butterflies. Butterflies go through a transformation that results in a beautiful creature, but it does not start out that way.

I am learning how to focus on the good instead of the bad.

 Finally, brethren, whatever things are true, whatever things are noble, whatever things are just, whatever things are pure, whatever things are lovely, whatever things are of good report, if there is any virtue and if there is anything praiseworthy—meditate on these things.

— PHILIPPIANS 4:8

One of the good things that I discovered is that I am not on this journey by myself. There are others who are on this path with me. There are some who have gone before me. Thank you for sharing your stories. Thank you for wiping my tears. Thank you for praying with me and for me. Thank you for encouraging me when I was in despair. Thank you for taking the time to read my journey.

As I share my journey, I pray that you develop hope as you recognize the power of God at work in my life is the same God who can do even more for you. For those of you who mourn, may you be comforted.

* * *

REFLECTION

What do you hope to gain from reading this book?

_____

_____

_____

_____

_____

_____

_____

_____

_____

_____

_____

_____

_____

_____

_____

_____

_____

_____

_____

_____

_____

_____

_____

_____

_____

_____

_____

_____

_____

_____

_____

_____

_____

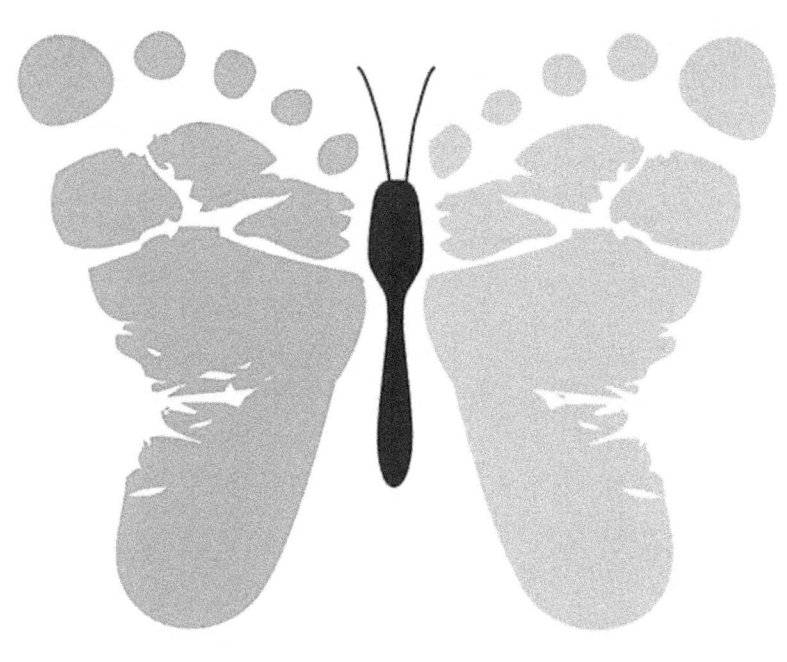

Scan below to listen to the opening section read by the author.

Infertility

/ĭn'fər-tĭl'ĭ-tē/: the inability to conceive after at least one year of unprotected sex

> *"The English language lacks the words to mourn an absence. For the loss of a parent, grandparent, spouse, child, or friend, we have all manner of words and phrases, some helpful some not. Still, we are conditioned to say something, even if it is only "I'm sorry for your loss." But for an absence, for someone who was never there at all, we are wordless to capture that particular emptiness. For those who deeply want children and are denied them, those missing babies hover like silent ephemeral shadows over their lives. Who can describe the feel of a tiny hand that is never held?"*

— Laura Bush, *Spoken From the Heart*

PRAYER

Father, I pray for those who long to have biological children. I pray for those who find themselves facing challenges in their pursuit of parenthood. Some have done all they know. Some have exhausted finances. Some of their bodies have taken the toll. Some of their minds are drained. Some of their spirits are weak. I ask in the strong name of Jesus that you would comfort and that you would encourage. I pray through the power of your Holy Spirit that you would provide peace that surpasses all understanding.

God, I ask that you provide revelation regarding any hindrances toward conception. I ask God in the strong name of Jesus that you would lead and provide the perfect path toward the desires of their heart to being a parent. Please grant the grace needed to endure this journey. In Jesus' Name. Amen.

* * *

REFLECTION

What answers do you desire from God?

_____

_____

_____

_____

_____

_____

_____

_____

_____

_____

_____

_____

_____

_____

_____

_____

_____

_____

_____

_____

_____

_____

_____

_____

_____

_____

_____

_____

Laying on of Hands

> *Is anyone among you sick? Let him call for the elders of the church, and let them pray over him, anointing him with oil in the name of the Lord. And the prayer of faith will save the sick, and the Lord will raise him up. And if he has committed sins, he will be forgiven. Confess your trespasses to one another, and pray for one another, that you may be healed. The effective, fervent prayer of a righteous man avails much.*
>
> — JAMES 5:14-16

D o you believe in prayer? Do you believe that God answers prayer? Do you know that you know that you know that God keeps His word? Well, let's keep it 100. I believe in prayer. I have seen God answer prayer time and time again. I believe what the Word of God says in the Bible. In James 5, a directive is given on how to assist someone who is dealing with sickness. The sick person is supposed to call for the elders of the church for prayer and anointing with oil. The prayer of faith will save the sick, and the Lord will raise him/her up. If sins were committed, they would be forgiven. We are also instructed to confess our trespasses to another and pray that we may be healed. The effective and fervent prayer avails much.

Is infertility a sickness? I would dare to say yes, it is. I have asked people to pray for me that I may be healed and able to conceive and carry a baby. My community also offered prayers that were unsolicited.

- In July 2011, I preached on the church's seventy-seventh anniversary. After the preaching moment, the bishop had the mothers of the church come and lay hands on me and pray for my physical healing.

- On September 18, 2011, the bishop called Michelle, Margo, and Sherrie to pray for me. They laid hands on me and travailed before the Lord on my behalf. He likened them to Hanna, Sarah, and Elizabeth.

- While visiting a church with our bishop, the apostle of the church called for two older women in his congregation to lay hands on me and pray on my behalf.

I must be honest and say the prayers were not answered as requested at that time. If you stick with me, you will discover in other chapters that God did answer their prayers in His own time. Physical healing did come forth—in *His* timing. Their prayers encouraged me and strengthened me. Their prayers helped me to hold out.

REFLECTION

Do you need to be healed? Are you sick? Have you asked someone to pray with you? Do you believe what the Word says in James 5:15–16?

* * *

Feel free to express your reflections creatively in the space below or on the following pages. Use words, images, colors, or any medium you prefer to document your thoughts and emotions. Let your creativity flow and capture your reflections in a way that feels authentic to you.

You're Next

> *Then he said, "About this time next year you shall embrace
> a son." And she said, "No, my lord. Man of God, do not lie
> to your maidservant?"*
>
> — 2 KINGS 4:16

Are you struggling with infertility? How many times have people smiled and said, "You're next"? For me, too many times to actually count. I know people are hopeful and are attempting to encourage me. I have even had the prophets come to me and say with certainty that I am next. I have also heard God is in the neighborhood. He's on your street. That may all be true, but I have not been next.

What do you do when "You are next" is predicted? What do you do when it appears as if you were given a false prophecy? What do you do when you succumb to "You're next," believe God's Word, and yet there is no child?

What do you do when other people who were not even travailing for a child become next? It makes me wonder. It makes me ask questions such as what happened to my spot in line? Why was I rooted? I know

11

God knows all, but why the delay? Some would say He is preparing me and my husband for the blessing, and we are not ready right now.

REFLECTION

What have people said to you regarding infertility that was hard to hear? How did you respond?

* * *

Feel free to express your reflections creatively in the space below or on the following pages. Use words, images, colors, or any medium you prefer to document your thoughts and emotions. Let your creativity flow and capture your reflections in a way that feels authentic to you.

You Said It; I Believe It

> *Everything I prophesied has come true, and now I will prophesy again. I will tell you the future before it happens.*
>
> — ISAIAH 42:9

God reveals Himself to us in many ways. We must have ears to hear and eyes to see what God is trying to show us. Over the course of my life, God has spoken in various ways. Primarily, I hear Him through dreams, by studying His Word, while listening to someone preach or teach, and through prophecy.

With regard to infertility and my desire to be a mom biologically, I believe God showed me the future before it happened so I would have hope. He knew the end before the beginning. He knew it would take years before my desire was fulfilled. He understood how I would feel, how I would respond, and what I would do in the interim. So in His wisdom and kindness, He shared words of prophecy through His sons and daughters.

I dreamt about Deja Joy. I saw a chocolate baby girl. In my dreams, we spent time at my grandmother's house. I held her, and I walked with her on the train.

God used a complete stranger to prophesy to me about having

17

twins. She told me that one of the children was hidden behind the other one.

I dreamt about Jalaam Justice. I was holding and talking to a chocolate baby boy. I told him his name and that it meant "hidden."

Our bishop spoke of "four sons" to my husband. During a sacred ceremony for our friend, God used the bishop to minister to me and lay hands on me. He told me that he too developed shingles during a period in his life when the Holy Spirit told him he was trying to do things himself. He told me I would conceive, and my children were going to be blessed.

A prophet prophesied that God was going to do for me what I prayed for others. I was blessed to have someone record this prophecy for me. I did not know this man, and he did not know me. He called me out by my first and last name in a room full of people. I used the words spoken to me that night for years. I used them to remind me and to remind God what He said.

I told God, "You said it, so I believe it." God was not like a man that He should lie. I told God, "You said it, so I believe it." You sent these people to me with these prophecies. I did not go out looking for them. I told God, "You said it, so I believe it."

REFLECTION

How do you hear God? What have you heard God say? Do you believe what He has said?

* * *

Feel free to express your reflections creatively in the space below or on the following pages. Use words, images, colors, or any medium you prefer to document your thoughts and emotions. Let your creativity flow and capture your reflections in a way that feels authentic to you.

Be Careful

> *So the Angel of the LORD said to Manoah, 'Of all that I said to the woman let her be careful. She may not eat anything that comes from the vine, nor may she drink wine or similar drink, nor eat anything unclean. All that I commanded her let her observe.'*
>
> — JUDGES 13:13–14

Have you ever wanted something so bad that you were willing to do whatever was necessary in order to get it? I can remember as a child wanting to go and hang out with my friends. My grandmother was old-school. On Saturday, the house had to be clean before you could go anywhere. I didn't even think about asking without cleaning my room, sweeping, mopping, dusting, and vacuuming the rest of the house. I understood Granny's expectations. I took care of my chores, and then I made my request.

I finally had an "aha!" moment while on this journey toward parenthood. I could not help but think from time to time, *What I did wrong? What did I do? What do I need to do?* Just like I would not dare to approach my granny without cleaning up her house, why did I feel comfortable doing so with God? God lent me this body. Have I been a good steward? What needs to be cleaned? What type of maintenance is needed to improve my health?

One of my fertility specialists encouraged me to exercise, change my diet, and deal with my stress. She helped me set a goal for weight and encouraged me to follow up with her when I reached my goal. She helped me see that I needed to be careful not only for my health, but also for the child I was hoping to carry.

The truth of the matter was I needed to be careful. It was time to deal with the truth. I needed to exercise, at least walk. Some of you may have heard me say before that I absolutely hate sweating, so running is a major challenge for me. Walking is a start though. I also needed to be careful with my blood pressure.

It was important for me to find ways to deal with stress in a healthy manner. I found out that quiet time with God worked for me. I often lit a candle and just sat quietly in the presence of God. I also needed to be careful with what I put in my body. It was time to change my diet. No more fast food, sweets, and soda. I needed a lifestyle change that included not only subtractions, but also additions of eating fruit and vegetables.

REFLECTION

What has God commanded you? How may you need to be careful? Are you willing to obey Him? For how long? What if you do not receive what you desire? Will you still be careful?

* * *

Feel free to express your reflections creatively in the space below or on the following pages. Use words, images, colors, or any medium you prefer to document your thoughts and emotions. Let your creativity flow and capture your reflections in a way that feels authentic to you.

I Believe

" *For with God nothing will be impossible.*

— LUKE 1:37

In my pursuit of answers after our first miscarriage, I found myself at a well-known clinic in the office of a well-known fertility specialist. I wanted answers, and I wanted help. Prior to this visit, I addressed the issue of fibroids by having a myomectomy. Basically, noncancerous growths in my uterus were surgically removed. The doctor was not certain whether the fibroids contributed to my miscarriage in 2007. Removing them would only increase my odds as space was freed up for the baby to attach and grow.

To say I was happy glad to try IVF is an understatement. The testing up to this point showed no problems with my husband's sperm nor my eggs. We started the process, which included taking medications in order to prepare my body for ovulation. The doctor would then remove my eggs so they could be fertilized. We were shocked to find out the doctor did not get any eggs during his attempt. After the failed egg retrieval, my husband and I went upstairs to talk with our physician. He too was disappointed. He ordered an MRI and asked me to return after he received the results.

The MRI showed that my uterus was clear except for a few small fibroids. The fallopian tubes were clear. His concern was for my uterus. It did not look healthy. After the myomectomy, the uterus should have shrunk, but mine was still enlarged. He was greatly concerned that I would not be able to carry a pregnancy to term. He suggested that I take an experimental drug to shrink the uterus and then do in vitro fertilization or have abdominal surgery to remove my eggs and fertilize them with my husband's sperm. We should have a gestational carrier carry our babies for us. His recommendation was to use a surrogate, which was very expensive.

I told him that I believed my uterus was strong enough to carry the pregnancy. I told him I would like to try in vitro again and implant the embryo in my own uterus. He told me he cannot move according to my beliefs or his own beliefs. He makes his decisions based on the facts and research.

Well, Doctor, it is a fact that the God that I serve is a Healer. He healed the woman with the issue of blood. It is a fact that Jesus raised Lazarus from the grave. It is a fact that nothing is impossible with God. These facts build my belief system. My beliefs direct my hope in a God who created me, so I certainly believe He can and will work all things together for my good so that I may conceive and carry the pregnancy.

REFLECTION

What do you believe? What do you believe about God?

* * *

Feel free to express your reflections creatively in the space below or on the following pages. Use words, images, colors, or any medium you prefer to document your thoughts and emotions. Let your creativity flow and capture your reflections in a way that feels authentic to you.

Endure the Process

> *For you have need of endurance, so that after you have done the will of God, you may receive the promise.*
>
> — HEBREWS 10:36

Have you ever been in the middle of something and then wondered to yourself if you made the right decision? That's how I feel whenever I get on a ride at an amusement park. I know that I do not enjoy the thrill. So why did I get on? Once you are on, you cannot get off. The rides only give me anxiety and an upset stomach. It would not be wise to jump off in the middle of the ride. I have no choice but to endure the process.

Sometimes the discomfort of the journey will cause us to want to get off the ride. We do not like how the journey makes us feel. We look around and see everyone else smiling and enjoying the ride (so we think).

Have you ever felt like quitting? Throwing in the towel? Well, I have. I was tired of people asking when we were going to have children. I was tired of hearing the prophecies and seeing no fulfillment. I was tired of dreaming. I was tired of feeling like I was the only one invested in conception (my husband had two sons before we married). I was tired of wondering if I had married the right man. Marriage was hard, and it was not getting any easier.

Let me go ahead and jump right in the water like I did when I married my spouse. We met in 2005. We were living in different cities. We talked on the phone every night until one of us fell asleep. Back then, cell phone minutes were free starting at 9:00 p.m. We couldn't wait to share what happened from the last time we spoke. I was sure God was telling me Marlon was the one. God gave both of us the same scripture when we went to church one Sunday morning. Two different preachers. Two different cities. One message. One scripture. God is doing a new thing!

 Behold, I will do a new thing, Now it shall spring forth; Shall you know it? I will even make a road in the wilderness and rivers in the desert.

— ISAIAH 43:19

Now honestly, I only meditated and focused on the first part of the scripture. I heard *new* and *now*. So we got married about three months later. I missed the part where God said He would make a road in the wilderness and rivers in the desert. Sounds like I missed the hardship and challenges of marriage. I missed that part, that part where I was given insight for endurance.

Yes, marriage was hard. Yes, dealing with infertility was hard. But that does not mean it was time to get off the ride. God was calling me to endure. If I stayed in His will, certainly I would behold His promise.

REFLECTION

What does enduring the process look like for you?

* * *

Feel free to express your reflections creatively in the space below or on the following pages. Use words, images, colors, or any medium you prefer to document your thoughts and emotions. Let your creativity flow and capture your reflections in a way that feels authentic to you.

Whatever It Takes

I endured two myomectomies in order to have fibroids removed
from my uterus. During the first surgery, a mass was discovered in
my left fallopian tube. My left tube was severed. It was later determined that the mass was a failed pregnancy. The doctor did not remove
the fibroids from inside my uterus, which was our greatest concern. This
happened in June 2008.

Two and half years later, in December 2010, the surgery was
repeated. This time, all the fibroids were removed. I had just started a
new teaching position. My recovery time was at least six weeks. I missed
about three weeks of work. I scheduled the procedure during the winter
break to decrease the number of missed days at work.

In March 2011, I returned to the fertility specialist and began
preparing for in vitro fertilization. I took numerous medications. I
injected myself with needles. I went to the doctor numerous times
throughout the week, sometimes back to back. Co-pays were due at each

visit. Some of my appointments could not be scheduled outside of work. Therefore, I missed more work without being paid. All my sick time was used up with the surgery.

In April 2011, I had surgery to remove my eggs. I awoke to my husband saying there weren't any eggs. I was confused and knew he had to be joking. What do you mean there weren't any eggs? He said the doctor had a hard time getting to my ovaries. They were high up in my abdomen. The doctor finally reached one of my ovaries, only to discover there were no eggs in the aspiration. How was that possible? All my testing and monitoring indicated there were follicles. Where were the eggs?

According to this doctor's facts and research, his recommendation was IVF with my eggs, my husband's sperm, and a stranger's uterus. We went in for a second opinion in the spring of 2012. She agreed with the first doctor. Her recommendation was a gestational carrier and a hysterectomy.

Up until this point in my journey, I had been willing to do "whatever" it took— surgery, missed work, missed income, physical pain and discomfort, mental anguish, frustration, looking and sounding like a fool when I proclaimed my belief in an invisible God!

REFLECTION

What does "whatever it takes" look like, sound like, feel like, and smell like? Are you willing to do whatever it takes?

* * *

Feel free to express your reflections creatively in the space below or on the following pages. Use words, images, colors, or any medium you prefer to document your thoughts and emotions. Let your creativity flow and capture your reflections in a way that feels authentic to you.

I'm Done

> *Trust in the Lord with all thy heart and lean not upon thy own understanding. In all thy ways acknowledge Him and He shall direct thy path.*
>
> — PROVERBS 3:5–6

M arlon and I got married in 2005. I never would have thought that we would have difficulty having children. It didn't make sense to me. We were doing it God's way, right? It seemed to me that the unmarried moms needed to give classes to the married women on how to get pregnant. I was obviously not doing something right. I didn't understand it.

During spring break of 2012, I went to see a new fertility specialist for a second opinion. I was ready to try in vitro fertilization again. She said she spent two days reviewing my records, trying to figure out what she could do to help me. Her conclusion was for me to have my uterus removed and then have a gestational carrier carry my child for me. My uterus was enlarged. It was preventing access to my eggs. Her other suggestion was that we adopt. According to her, the most important thing was that we have a family, and the route was not important, just the outcome.

After leaving her office, I was devastated. I never contemplated being told a hysterectomy was part of the remedy. There was such a strong desire to carry my own child. Yes, there were other options with regard to having children, but were they my options? According to her, that was it. I should just be done with it and move on.

Well, I didn't agree with her conclusion. I was not ready to be done. I was not ready to move on.

My husband and I decided I would not do anything else medically. Lupron was still available. By taking it, it could possibly shrink the uterus, thus making it healthy enough to carry a baby and provide access to the eggs. I decided to leave well enough alone and trust God to do it His way. I expected God to work a miracle. I was done with trying to understand. I was done with trying to work it out. Done.

REFLECTION

Infertility can be challenging in many ways. How has infertility affected you? Has it affected you mentally, physically, financially, socially, emotionally? Do you fully and completely trust God?

Complete this sentence:

Today, I'm done _____ .

* * *

Feel free to express your reflections creatively in the space below or on the following pages. Use words, images, colors, or any medium you prefer to document your thoughts and emotions. Let your creativity flow and capture your reflections in a way that feels authentic to you.

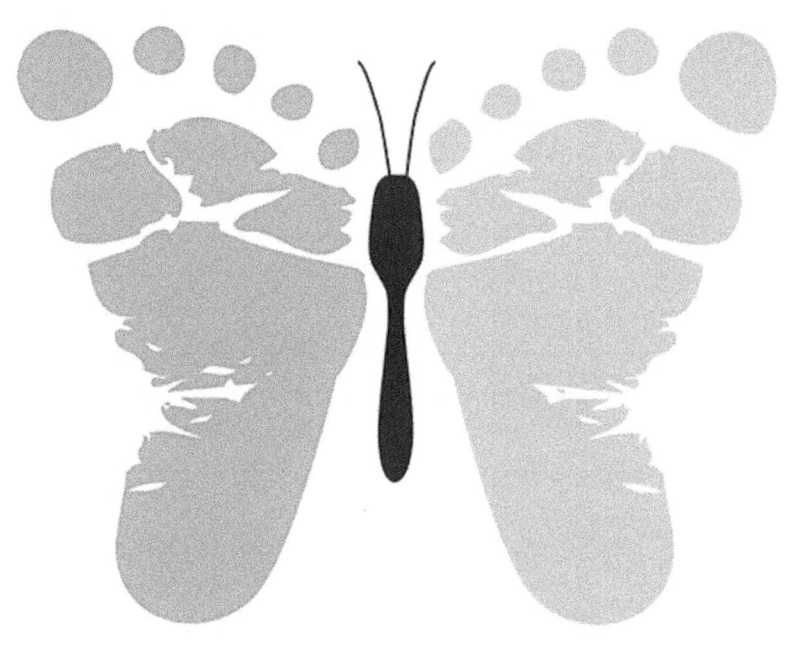

Scan below to listen to the opening section read by the author.

Miscarriage

/mis-kar-ij/: the loss of a pregnancy prior to twenty weeks gestation

> *"I didn't feel anything at first when Miss Ethel told me,
> but now I think about it all the time. It's like there's a
> baby girl down here waiting to be born. She's some-
> where close by in the air, in this house, and she picked
> me to be born to. And now she has to find some other
> mother."* Cece began to sob.

> *"Come on girl. Don't cry,"* whispered Frank.

> *"Why not? I can be miserable if I want to. You don't need
> to try and make it go away. It shouldn't go away. It's
> just as sad as it ought to be and I'm not going to hide
> from what's true just because it hurts."*

— Toni Morrison, *Home*

PRAYER

God, I am praying for the parent who is hurting and having a hard time dealing with the reality that their child is no longer here. To carry a child and to have the child leave too soon is a burden that is hard to bear. Gone with the child are the dreams of the future.

Comfort those whose hearts still ache. Provide peace for those who still question. Please send forth healing physically, mentally, and spiritually. In Jesus' Name. Amen.

* * *

REFLECTION

What answers do you desire from God?

_____

_____

_____

_____

_____

_____

_____

_____

_____

_____

_____

_____

_____

_____

_____

_____

_____

_____

_____

_____

_____

_____

_____

_____

_____

_____

_____

_____

_____

Protect Your Promise

> *Now after those days his wife Elizabeth conceived; and she hid herself five months, saying, "Thus the Lord has dealt with me, to take away my reproach among people."*
>
> — LUKE 1:24–25

I always wanted to be a mother. I looked forward to getting pregnant and sharing a child with my husband.

In December 2007, we conceived. I was ecstatic. We told everyone who would listen as our village waited in expectation too. We were often asked when we were going to have a baby. I can remember sharing my good news with my granny, only to have her question whether we were ready to be parents to another child since my husband was a father to two sons prior to us marrying. I was saddened and disappointed that she did not share in my joy.

I went to my first obstetrician appointment, and it was confirmed that we were pregnant. I was scheduled for a twelve-week appointment on Valentine's Day. I was so excited about this appointment. We would be able to hear our baby's heartbeat.

The doctor came in with the Doppler machine and could not find the baby's heartbeat. She went to get someone else to assist her. This doctor could not find the heartbeat either. They rolled in an ultrasound machine to confirm their thoughts. There was no heartbeat. There was a sac, but it was empty. The plan was to continue with blood draws to ensure the HCG levels were decreasing. At some point, my body would naturally miscarry.

I was a woman of great faith. I needed and wanted the doctors to be wrong. I needed and wanted God to work a miracle. I promised Him I would make sure He would get all the glory if He just turned this around for us. At first, it looked like He was going to do just that. The numbers went up instead of down. Days and days went by without any bleeding. And then the levels went down, and the bleeding and cramping started.

A couple of weeks later, I found myself in worship preparing to lead our congregation in prayer. All of a sudden, I had an urgent need to go to the bathroom. To my disappointment, my precious child passed right into the toilet. I wailed and cried and wailed and cried. I could not believe God was allowing this to happen to me. I was the faithful one. I was the married one. I was the one who prayed and believed for others. I was the one who was doing it God's way. Why would He allow this to happen to me?

My best friend fought her way into that small bathroom stall with me, and we said goodbye to my child. We said goodbye to what would not be. We said goodbye to ended dreams that did not have the opportunity to even start.

I did my best to get myself together and made it back in the sanctuary just in time to pray. Though I desperately needed someone to pray for me, I remember very clearly praying a prayer of thanksgiving even though I felt like my heart had been ripped apart.

It was so challenging to tell people that the pregnancy had ended. We never fully explained the situation to our son, Macaiah, who was five years old at the time. I came to the conclusion that we revealed the pregnancy too early on. We never thought the pregnancy would not go forth without hindrance or complication. We never even considered the possibility that we would miscarry. It was never an option. It was never a thought in our minds.

I spent a lot of time trying to determine my fault in all this. What did I do wrong? What should I have done that I did not do? A prophet of God later told me that someone had been praying against my conception. Should I have kept our pregnancy a secret? Did I open the door to curses because I shared our good news? Did I put my child at risk? Did I protect my promise?

I had a better understanding as to why Elizabeth may have hidden herself during the first five months of pregnancy. She was attempting to protect her promise. It took years for me to realize the miscarriage was not my fault. It took years for me to accept that which I could not understand. It took years for me to acknowledge I was a good mother, and I protected my promise until she was no longer a promise.

REFLECTION

Give examples of how you have attempted to protect your promises. Were you successful? Do you blame yourself for failures or unexpected events?

Consider writing a letter to your child. What would you say?

Consider writing a letter to God about your promise. What would you say?

* * *

Feel free to express your reflections creatively in the space below or on the following pages. Use words, images, colors, or any medium you prefer to document your thoughts and emotions. Let your creativity flow and capture your reflections in a way that feels authentic to you.

Not Again

> Bear one another's burdens, and so fulfill the law of Christ.
>
> — GALATIANS 6:2

I have been sharing deeply and honestly. Is it okay if I can continue to do so? Can we keep it real? If not, you may want to stop reading and choose something else to occupy your time because I have to be honest and spill all the beans. There are some times when I do not want to minister. There are some times when I do not feel like serving. There have been times when I did not like my assignment.

I have found myself asking how many times must I minister to women who become pregnant and are not happy about it? Not again. I have found myself asking why am I called to walk alongside women and young teenagers who have made decisions to terminate their pregnancy? Not again. I have found myself asking why are they permitted to conceive and then given the freedom to end the child's life? Not again.

How many times must I minister to women who complain about their pregnancy? *I'm gaining weight. I'm so sick. What are we going to do? How are we going to take care of this child? We are too old to be parents again.*

Often there are so many complaints and very few acknowledgments of how truly blessed they are to be expecting a child. I made a vow based off these experiences. I will not complain while I am pregnant. When God blesses me with what I request, I will be grateful.

REFLECTION

How do you help bear someone else's burden? Is it ever difficult to do so? Please elaborate.

* * *

Feel free to express your reflections creatively in the space below or on the following pages. Use words, images, colors, or any medium you prefer to document your thoughts and emotions. Let your creativity flow and capture your reflections in a way that feels authentic to you.

It's Party Time... Again

> *Rejoice with those who rejoice, and weep with those who weep.*
>
> — ROMANS 12:15

In 2011, I was busy, busy, busy rejoicing about new life that was soon to arrive in the earth. I was happy glad that women all around me were pregnant. I found myself covering them in prayer asking God to keep both mom and baby in good health. I also became an expert at baby showers. That year, I helped plan four baby showers.

Two of these showers were for my best friend and sister, Michelle. We had hopes to conceive and actually share our pregnancies together. When I endured my miscarriage in 2008, Michelle walked with me. She let me share my pain, and we suffered together. We also wanted to share the joys of pregnancy together. When conception was not happening for either of us, I changed my prayer and asked God not to delay her gift because of me, but send forth her blessing speedily. He did just that, and Zoe was born healthy in August 2011.

The third baby shower was for another expecting mom who was in her forties when she conceived. She and her husband were not expecting this. They were actually planning for her husband's retirement. They were not ecstatic at first. They were very concerned about their ability to provide for this child so late in life.

The fourth baby shower was for a coworker who complained every time I asked her about her pregnancy and even the times I did not. She volunteered to inform me how sick she was and how she just could not wait to deliver the child. I vowed not to complain when God sends my child into the earth. I had to check myself when in the presence of these women and praise God for their blessings.

After that year, I was partied out. I found myself gracefully bowing out of baby showers and children's birthday parties. I realized I was easily triggered with emotions of anger and sadness when invited to baby showers of young women who were not married. Instead of attending the party, I decided to pray for a healthy pregnancy and safe delivery for the mom and child.

REFLECTION

Identify a time it may have been difficult rejoicing with others. What made it difficult?

* * *

Feel free to express your reflections creatively in the space below or on the following pages. Use words, images, colors, or any medium you prefer to document your thoughts and emotions. Let your creativity flow and capture your reflections in a way that feels authentic to you.

Dreams

As I stated in a previous chapter, God speaks to me through dreams. There are many ways that we can, and I do hear God. He often uses dreams to show me something in the future. Sometimes what I see requires a petition to God for mercy, healing, and protection. Some of my dreams are ways that God gives me hope and reassurance that He has heard my prayers. I just need to hold out and wait for manifestation of the promise.

- I dreamt I was pregnant. I was at the hospital in a gown running and jumping in the hallway. I seemed to know that the nurse was going to still say I was not ready to push because I was not fully dilated.

- I dreamt I was in the hospital. I was in a room with two pregnant women on either side of me. I was in the bed, in a gown, hooked up to an IV. I was waiting on Marlon, my husband, to come back. I was not sure where he was, but I thought he left to get something to eat.

- I dreamt I was at Granny's house packing up a truck. There was a jumper on the porch for twins, though only one of the twins was in the jumper.

- Lady Lisa called me in March 2012. She had a dream that Marlon was carrying a baby girl. She was about five months old. She was light-skinned and had curly hair. In the dream, she kept asking Marlon if this was Deja Joy. My response was "This is our baby girl." She wanted to know why I did not tell her I was pregnant. Everyone in her backyard gathered around us. We were very happy.

- I dreamt I was decorating my office in our home for a baby girl. The walls were pink. There was a crib and a large blanket that said "Thank heaven for little girls."

As I reflect on each of these dreams, I can see how in some way, each has come to pass. God is amazing! Everything we see in the dream may not come to pass as we saw it. If we pay attention and allow the Holy Spirit to provide revelation, we would be in awe of what God is showing us.

REFLECTION

What dreams, prophecies, or visions are you waiting on?

* * *

Feel free to express your reflections creatively in the space below or on the following pages. Use words, images, colors, or any medium you prefer to document your thoughts and emotions. Let your creativity flow and capture your reflections in a way that feels authentic to you.

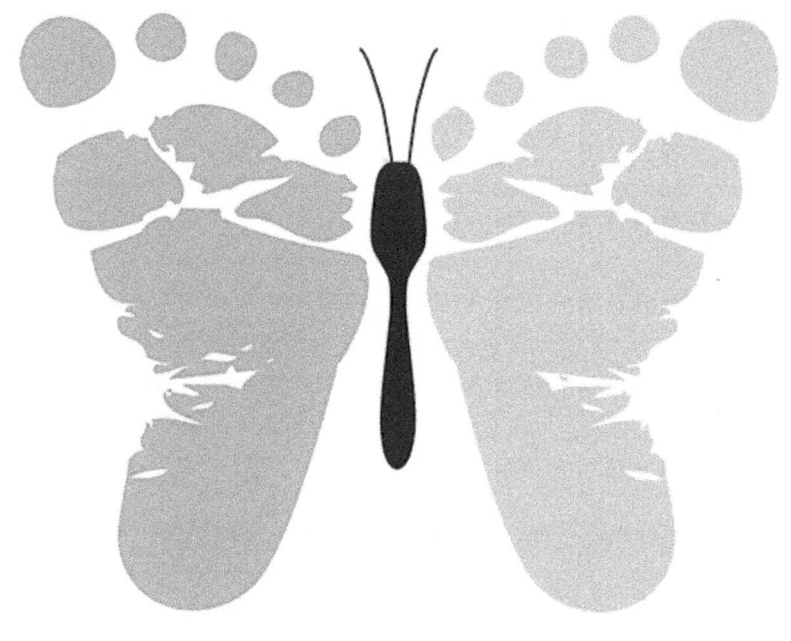

Scan below to listen to the opening section read by the author.

Stillbirth

/stil-ˌbərth/: when a baby dies in the womb after twenty weeks of gestation

"Thinking back, it was such a surreal day; when I wasn't sitting or crying I slowly paced the house like a zombie, waiting and weeping. I did not watch TV, read or listen to the radio. I was just "there," thinking too much. Our old life, the one that included and was planned around the son we were fervently awaiting, was over. Our new life, the one where we had to learn to live without him, had not yet begun. We were in limbo. He was gone but he was with us. Was I still pregnant? I surely looked pregnant, but my baby was no longer alive inside of me, and I carried him inside of me not because of courage or dedication, but because I had to."

— Silvia Corradin, *Losing Alex: The Night I Held an Angel*

PRAYER

Father, thank you for the gift of life. We thank you for the possibility of being a parent. We ask now that your Holy Spirit would be a comforter. We ask that you would be our Healer. Please help us as we struggle with the pain of this loss—the loss of our precious child. The loss of possibilities. The loss of relationships. The loss of dreams that will never be manifested. Help us in our moments of lacking understanding. Help us to accept your will. To lose a child this late in pregnancy is hard. So though we grieve, we also rejoice that this child was *still born*. In Jesus' Name. Amen.

* * *

REFLECTION

What answers do you desire from God?

_____

_____

_____

_____

_____

_____

_____

_____

_____

_____

_____

_____

_____

_____

_____

_____

_____

_____

_____

_____

_____

_____

_____

_____

_____

_____

_____

_____

_____

_____

_____

_____

_____

_____

It Is Well

> *And he said:*
>   *"Naked I came from my mother's womb,*
>   *And naked shall I return there.*
>   *The Lord gave, and the Lord has taken away;*
>   *Blessed be the name of the Lord."*
>
> — JOB 1:21

After twelve years of marriage and struggles with infertility, we finally delivered a healthy baby boy in March 2018. Though we were elated and though we were grateful, this was not the child I saw in my dreams. She was chocolate brown with two little afro puffs. I was confident that Deja Joy was still going to make her appearance in the earth.

After discussing this with my husband and praying, we tried IVF again. This pregnancy was different. There was more peace. My blood pressure was not an issue like the first time. I enjoyed the pregnancy along with the other children. We spent many days expressing our joy and thanksgiving by blowing bubbles.

During Father's Day weekend, I started to feel sick. My symptoms were similar to having the flu. I just felt sick. I was nauseated. I had body aches. Just felt yucky. I didn't want to be labeled as a hypochondriac, so I ignored how I felt. I had an upcoming doctor's appointment and planned to address it then.

As I sat in the waiting room, I asked myself when was the last time I felt Deja Joy move. I couldn't remember. Before I could think much more about it, my name was called for my ultrasound. The sonographer asked about my weekend. I told her about not feeling well, and then she said she would be right back. Something told me that was not good and something was wrong. When I asked her if something was wrong, she said she needed to get a doctor to come and look at the ultrasound. I reached for my cell phone and called my husband. The sonographer returned with the doctor, who confirmed there was no heartbeat. I was devastated and shocked. I wailed and cried. I had no words to express the pain I felt in that moment. I could hear myself praying in tongues. It was as if I was having an out-of-body experience, and I was watching myself respond to this horrible news. I was sent home to wait and see how my doctor wanted to proceed.

I was scheduled for a C-section the following Friday. I packed clothes for Deja Joy. To be quite honest with you, I was still hoping for a miracle. When we arrived at the hospital, I insisted on a team member from the NICU to be present during the delivery. What if God worked a miracle? What if she was born alive? I did not want to waste any time waiting on the cavalry. I needed the cavalry to already be in the room.

My surgery was challenging. I lost a lot of blood. The doctors had great difficulty getting Deja Joy out of my uterus. I ended up in the ICU. The whole experience was bad. This included poor care and an incision that did not heal until four months later.

Our whole village was in anticipation of Deja Joy's arrival. We had just celebrated with a virtual baby shower with our friends and family. Her death affected more than our immediate family. Everyone needed time to process the loss and grieve her death. We celebrated Deja Joy's life with a graveside service. We had a bubble machine and passed out bubbles to our family and friends to symbolize the joy she brought to each of us. We were able to share beautiful pictures of her. The nurses dressed her in the outfits I had brought and took beautiful pictures.

At some point, my husband and I were able to say, "It is well."

Despite the pain in our hearts. Despite the need to pivot. Despite the questions we still had. Despite feeling betrayed and abandoned. *It is well*. God was still the boss. God was still a good, good Father. God blessed us with her for thirty-three weeks. We experienced undeniable joy through her living. *It is well*.

Embrace the Joy I Left Behind
(an Ode to Deja Joy)

I can see the tears in your eyes - I am sorry that you had to cry
But if you take a minute to look, you will see that you can embrace
the joy I left behind

Mom and Dad I love you most
Know that I heard every prayer you prayed and every plan you made
Even through-out these 15 years that it seemed the dream was delayed
You stayed hopeful that a miracle was soon to be made
Though the road at times was difficult you abided your time
Spreading your love to others - Unconditional
Love beyond measure – a true treasure

Dad I loved our quiet times alone when mommy was asleep
You talking to her belly was our secret to keep – gentle I love you's
transmitting through space and time
Don't worry you will always be forever mine

Mom the sound of your heart beat will forever be my favorite melody
Even the moments I heard you cry was comforting to me
like the moon in the night sky - In your dreams I will be
where we can still have times I like to call Mommy & Me
Though barrettes you will not have to put in my hair –
know that a crown of promise still rest there

Please tell my siblings that I love and miss them too,
and that I hope they find all of their missing shoes
I'm sorry I won't be able to do all of the annoying things that little sister's do
But we will meet again, trust me this is true

But until that day comes I hope they have fun in the tub
Tons of fun in the sun, lady bugs & Butterflies
and that they give each other lots and lots of hugs
Knowing that each time they hug each other – they are hugging me
Creating an atmosphere of jubilee - Embracing the joy I left behind

I'm glad to see all of my aunties & uncles there by your side
I can see the tears in their eyes
knowing they were waiting to hold me in their arms,
spoil me with dolls and sweet treats
Plans of birthday parties and tickling my feet
These feet that have left an imprint on so many hearts
Even though after 31 weeks I had to say goodbye
The joy I left you can never be denied
Within those 31 weeks I left a mark & I did my part
For I am the promise manifested - I gave hope to the hopeless
I am a gift of Faith renewed that all things are possible
I created joy!
For joy is the settled assurance that God was in control of all
the details of my life*
Deja means: already seen - it's a feeling that you have already experienced
– a remembrance
It is something that is happing now
The quiet confidence that ultimately everything is going to be alright*
The determined choice to praise God even in this situation
The declaration to still have joy!

So quiet your minds and Don't lose sight that God is in our midst
Wiping our tears, giving us courage, and strengthening our hearts
I just need you to promise me that you will
Continue to Embrace the Joy I left behind

Written in love by Auntie ButterflyPoet
Except from author Rick Warren

Scan below to listen to the poem being read.

Ode to Deja Joy

REFLECTION

Has there ever been a time when it was hard for you to bless the Lord? Is it possible for things to be well while suffering a major loss in your life?

* * *

Feel free to express your reflections creatively in the space below or on the following pages. Use words, images, colors, or any medium you prefer to document your thoughts and emotions. Let your creativity flow and capture your reflections in a way that feels authentic to you.

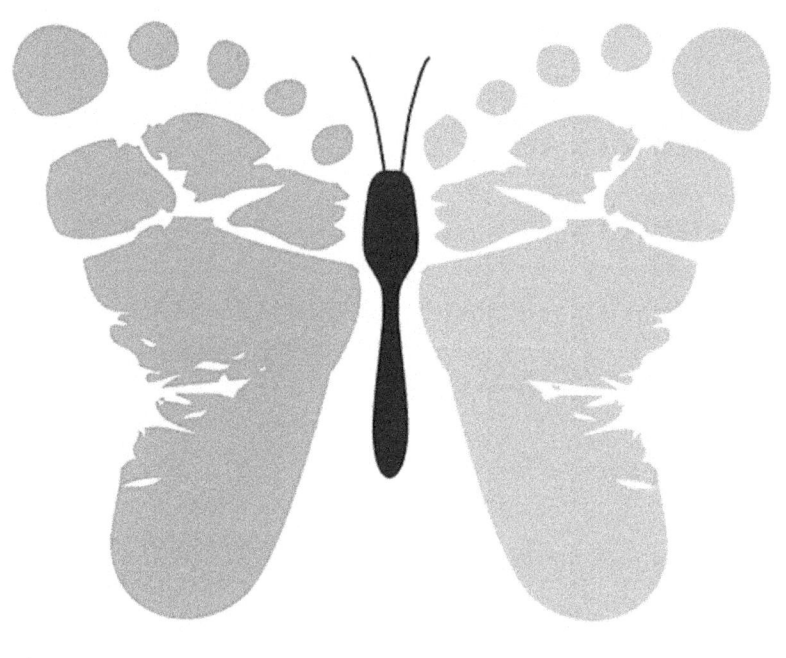

Scan below to listen to the opening section read by the author.

Joy

/joi/: being content, no matter your circumstances

"Joy is the settled assurance that God is in control of all the details of my life, the quiet confidence that ultimately everything is going to be alright and the determined choice to praise God in every situation."

— Rick Warren

PRAYER

Father, this journey to being a parent has been full of unexpected paths. There have been moments of shock, disappointment, anger, and pain. There have also been moments of laughter, growth, and faith-building. Through it all, You have been present to love and support us. And for that, we are grateful.

Holy Spirit, please help us to choose JOY no matter what is and whatever is not. Help us to choose life, an abundant life that is full of JOY. In Jesus' Name. Amen.

* * *

REFLECTION

What answers do you desire from God?

_____
_____
_____
_____
_____
_____
_____
_____
_____
_____
_____
_____
_____
_____
_____
_____
_____
_____
_____
_____
_____
_____
_____
_____
_____
_____
_____
_____
_____
_____
_____

There Must Be A Better Way

"Now Naaman, commander of the army of the king of Syria, was a great and honorable man in the eyes of his master, because by him the Lord had given victory to Syria. He was also a mighty man of valor, but a leper.

And the Syrians had gone out on raids, and had brought back captive a young girl from the land of Israel. She waited on Naaman's wife. Then she said to her mistress, "If only my master were with the prophet who is in Samaria! For he would heal him of his leprosy." And Naaman went in and told his master, saying, "Thus and thus said the girl who is from the land of Israel."

Then the king of Syria said, "Go now, and I will send a letter to the king of Israel."

So he departed and took with him ten talents of silver, six thousand shekels of gold, and ten changes of clothing. Then he brought the letter to the king of Israel, which said,

Now be advised, when this letter comes to you, that I have sent Naaman my servant to you, that you may heal him of his leprosy.

And it happened, when the king of Israel read the letter, that he tore his clothes and said, "Am I God, to kill

*and make alive, that this man sends a man to me to heal
him of his leprosy? Therefore please consider, and see how he
seeks a quarrel with me."*

*So it was, when Elisha the man of God heard that the
king of Israel had torn his clothes, that he sent to the king,
saying, "Why have you torn your clothes? Please let him
come to me, and he shall know that there is a prophet in
Israel."*

*Then Naaman went with his horses and chariot, and
he stood at the door of Elisha's house. And Elisha sent a
messenger to him, saying, "Go and wash in the Jordan seven
times, and your flesh shall be restored to you, and you shall
be clean." But Naaman became furious, and went away
and said, "Indeed, I said to myself, 'He will surely come out
to me, and stand and call on the name of the Lord his God,
and wave his hand over the place, and heal the leprosy.' Are
not the Abanah and the Pharpar, the rivers of Damascus,
better than all the waters of Israel? Could I not wash in
them and be clean?" So he turned and went away in a rage.*

*And his servants came near and spoke to him, and said,
"My father, if the prophet had told you to do something
great, would you not have done it? How much more then,
when he says to you, 'Wash, and be clean'?" So he went
down and dipped seven times in the Jordan, according to
the saying of the man of God; and his flesh was restored like
the flesh of a little child, and he was clean.*

— 2 KINGS 5:1–14

I always wanted to be a mom. When I ran into physical challenges that delayed my ability to conceive and give birth, I recalled a strong desire to want to be a foster parent as a child. My husband agreed that we could check it out and see what, if anything, would become of it. The process of getting approved was so much more than we realized.

In March 2012, I took the training to become a foster parent for medically fragile children. Marlon completed all his hours in April. It seems it took forever and a day to complete the requirements. We had to provide so much paperwork. There were things in our past that needed to be explained. We had to wait for openings to take first aid and CPR training. We asked our friend to complete a recommendation for us. He agreed. We gave him the form in March, and as of July, it had still not been returned. Our son did not want to go to the doctor for the physical. If it wasn't this, it was that.

The whole process left me saying there must be a better way. Yes, I longed to be a mother. Yes, I wanted to fulfill my purpose. Yes, I wanted to meet the needs of a child who needed a family. Was it necessary to have strangers picking and prodding in our life? Was it necessary to rely on others to help us in the process when obviously they were not equally concerned with deadlines? There must be a better way.

REFLECTION

It is quite possible to develop expectations regarding our journey. We imagine how things will go. Oftentimes, things do not transpire the way we thought it would. What do you do when this happens? Can you identify with the statement "there must be a better way"? Please explain.

* * *

Feel free to express your reflections creatively in the space below or on the following pages. Use words, images, colors, or any medium you prefer to document your thoughts and emotions. Let your creativity flow and capture your reflections in a way that feels authentic to you.

Don't Postpone Joy

> *You will show me the path of life;*
> *In Your presence is fullness of joy;*
> *At Your right hand are pleasures forevermore.*

> — PSALM 16:11

In 2012, we were licensed as a foster care home. We were happy glad about it. The agency that we worked with had a medically fragile program. We agreed to bring into our home children who had special needs for various reasons. We also agreed that the children would stay with us as long as God desired. Some would stay for a day and others for a lifetime.

I am so glad that something shifted in my thinking. My aha! moment encouraged me to stop focusing on what I did not have and instead focus on what I did have. Yes, I still desired being a mom biologically. Instead of using my energy on that desire, I chose instead to make myself available to use my gifts with children who were here now. Let me share just a few of the children who came to our home and left memories we will never forget.

Our first placement was in April 2013. He stayed with us for two months. He brought us pure joy. His medical needs were many, but

God. We watched him flourish and improve in ways the medial professionals did not expect.

In July of that year, Parrish joined our family. Her plan was adoption. We learned of her in December. She became so ill, we were not permitted to visit her. I will never forget my first visits with her. She was not impressed with me. I went in to see her. I knelt down to say hi, and she rolled to the other side of the bed. When I walked around to the other side, she rolled over to the other side of the bed. Her only interest was Care Bears.

When my husband and son came to visit her for the first time, she lit up. To see her laugh and smile made me laugh and smile. Her discharge meeting was so grim. I left afraid to bring her home, fearing she would die. The doctors were unsure whether she would walk, talk, eat, or drink. She had developmental delays and would need various forms of therapy. We accepted our assignment and brought Parrish home. She was eighteen months old, and now she is eleven years old. We have watched God heal her in ways that were not expected. She is walking, talking, running, and drinking.

Sofia came to us straight from the hospital. Her plan was reunification with her family. She had an older sister who wanted custody of her. We took her to visits with her sister and knew from the beginning what the outcome would be. This did not change the way we loved and provided for her. She was a part of our family in every way. Our friends and family embraced and loved her. Having her in our life was such a pleasure that I could not bear the thought of her leaving us. When we were given the date she would go with her sister, I cried and cried out to the Lord. In my mind, our home was the best place for her. In my mind, a two-parent family was best. In my mind, I knew better than God what was best for Sofia.

The weeks leading up to her leaving were rough. I grieved like never before in anticipation of our loss. Sofia's sister was such a blessing to us the day we left her at court forever. She asked us if we would be willing to be Sofia's Godparents and stay connected in her life. We of course said yes.

Not many days later, we received a call for a placement of twins. God knew exactly what we needed. If Sofia remained with us, there would not have been room in our home for two placements. They were in the NICU. One of them was ready for discharge, and the other would probably be ready in about a week. We had a trip planned for my birthday. We were interested, but the timing was off. The placement coordinator was able to convince them we were the best option for the babies and to postpone their discharge until after our trip. When the nurses met me, they confessed their hesitancy and concerns regarding the babies. Meeting me reassured them that they were being placed with a family that would take good care of them. Unfortunately, they had bad experiences with children being placed with people who had ill intent.

I enjoyed every part of being their mom, from midnight feedings to crawling, walking, and talking. Right when it looked like all was well, we were informed that a cousin inquired about getting them. Once again, my heart was broken. I just knew these boys would be a part of our lives forever. Not only were they leaving, but they were also moving away to New York. I received a gift from their new mother, Davina. She always acknowledges me as their mama. She always acknowledges my husband as their dad. The twins understand that they have five parents who love them. Davina, in her kindness, sent me pictures almost daily. I was able to see and hear them. She helped make the transition so much easier for both the children and our family. The twins are eight years old now, and we are still connected. I am so grateful to be a part of their lives and watch them grow and mature.

Brayden and Athena came to our home in March 2017. They were separate placements. Brayden's plan was reunification, and Athena's plan was adoption. They both are Robinsons today. We were only able to take them in as placements because we let go of the twins.

I learned a lot from fostering. God taught me how to love and let go. While the children are in our care, we have a responsibility to love them in every way that is needed. We provide, we nurture, we model, and we discipline. When and if God says it's time for them to leave, then we must let them go. We have to trust His plan and remember He sees the end from the beginning. So while they are with us, we enjoy every moment with grateful hearts.

REFLECTION

Identify when you may have postponed joy. Write or draw a picture of this.

* * *

Feel free to express your reflections creatively in the space below or on the following pages. Use words, images, colors, or any medium you prefer to document your thoughts and emotions. Let your creativity flow and capture your reflections in a way that feels authentic to you.

In the Meantime

> *Delight yourself also in the Lord,*
> *And He shall give you the desires of your heart.*
>
> — PSALM 37:4

What do you do while you are waiting? Many of us have learned how to multitask, which can be good or bad. For example, cooking dinner. Yesterday, I made green beans, macaroni and cheese, and baked turkey legs. I started my dinner by boiling water for the macaroni. While waiting, I put on the smoked turkey for the green beans. I then fed my four little ones snacks. I hooked my other child up for her G-tube feeding. I washed a few dishes. When my phone dinged, I checked the notifications. I try to use my time wisely. I have other responsibilities other than cooking dinner. It would not be wise to just work on one element of the dinner at a time.

Well, while waiting for God to fulfill his promise for me to be a mother biologically, I began to focus on other responsibilities. In the meantime, we fostered numerous children, of which three of them are a permanent part of our family. In the meantime, I worked as a child development teacher. In the meantime, I served in my local church as an elder. In the meantime, it is important to keep moving forward as you wait—and it would be nice if you waited with joy and expectancy.

REFLECTION

What are you waiting on? How's the wait going? In the *meantime*, how could you improve your waiting?

* * *

Feel free to express your reflections creatively in the space below or on the following pages. Use words, images, colors, or any medium you prefer to document your thoughts and emotions. Let your creativity flow and capture your reflections in a way that feels authentic to you.

God Is with Us

> The Lord remembers us and will bless us:
>   He will bless his people Israel,
>   he will bless the house of Aaron.
>
> — PSALM 115:12

After many years of infertility, numerous myomectomies, a miscarriage, ectopic pregnancy, and negative reports from doctors, which included advising a hysterectomy, I was introduced to Dr. Garcia. My brain could not let go of the thought that there were other ways to get to my ovaries other than vaginally. When I mentioned this to my fertility specialist, she said she knew of only one person who did it, and he was retiring soon. I will never forget meeting him. After reviewing my case, he said with his strong accent, "Mrs. Robinson, your case is challenging, but I am willing to try." Thank God for the *but*!

This pregnancy began with a Word God spoke to me at a conference. He said, "Try again" like the men who were fishing all night and had caught nothing. At Jesus's Word, we tried again. We began the process of in vitro. We found out we were pregnant on my husband's birthday. This held such great significance for us as God kept reminding us that He remembered us and that He would bless us.

The pregnancy was full of challenges and concerns. My blood pressure remained elevated. There were a few times where they could not find the baby or his heartbeat on the ultrasound. I bled almost every day of the pregnancy. I had to remind myself that all was well even though I saw blood. I had to remind myself that God was faithful to keep His word. I could not function according to my senses—what I saw, felt, heard, smelled, or tasted. I had to walk by faith and know that I know that I know that God was with us.

At the beginning of March, we had an amazing baby shower. This was our community's opportunity to give thanks to God with us for our precious miracle. We told the whole story. Many did not know that it took almost thirteen years for us to behold our first biological child together. Many did not know the ups and downs that came with infertility. Many did not know that we used IVF in order to conceive. We made sure that God received all the glory for our miracle who was soon to arrive.

His due date was April 4. I started seeing the obstetrician multiple times a week in order to monitor my blood pressure and the baby's progress. I spent a weekend in the hospital so they could keep a closer eye on Malachi. A few days later, I went in for a nonstress test, and there were some concerns with his responsiveness. Additionally, I lost fluid from the last time the test was completed. I was admitted for monitoring again.

On Sunday morning, the covering doctor came in to tell me we could go home. The baby was looking good on the monitor, and the amniotic fluid had stabilized. She advised me to return in the morning to repeat the tests. As I sat there with the nurse preparing to go home, something just did not feel right. As she took the IV out, I asked her if I could just have thirty minutes before leaving. She left to tell the doctor I wanted more time before agreeing to go home. The nurse was right back in the room. She began giving me directives stating she believed the baby was having heart decelerations. The midwife came in to check and confirmed the baby's heart rate was dangerously low.

They rushed me into the operating room to do an emergency C-section. I had just enough time to call my husband before my bed was being pushed down the hall. Everyone was in a panic. The person carrying the surgical instruments dropped them on the floor. The anesthesiologist was inquiring about why I did not have an IV. All I could do was pray and ask God to be present in the midst of all the chaos.

When I woke up, the obstetrician was there to tell me what happened. She told us that my abdomen filled with blood as soon as she made the first cut. It was difficult for her to see. She could not find the baby, and she was running out of time. Time was quickly reaching the point of life and death. She said she always wondered if there was a God. Now she knows there is. The doctor told us she felt a force take control of her hands. She was led to the baby and was able to pull him out of my uterus. I lost seven liters of blood and required observation in the ICU.

The baby weighed four pounds and seven ounces and was eighteen inches long. He spent eight days in the hospital and came home on my birthday. We named him Malachi Immanuel, Malachi because he was a messenger of God even before he left my womb, and Immanuel because God used this child as a daily reminder that He was with us.

REFLECTION

What evidence do you have that God is with you?

* * *

Feel free to express your reflections creatively in the space below or on the following pages. Use words, images, colors, or any medium you prefer to document your thoughts and emotions. Let your creativity flow and capture your reflections in a way that feels authentic to you.

Won't He Do It Again!

> *Now to Him who is able to do exceedingly abundantly above all that we ask or think, according to the power that works in us.*
>
> — EPHESIANS 3:20

After delivering Malachi, I could not stop thinking about the baby girl I saw in my dreams. When we were pregnant with Malachi, I just knew he was the little girl we had been waiting for. Boy, was I wrong! I felt strongly that we should try IVF again and see if Deja Joy would manifest. And that she did. I enjoyed carrying her. I had unspeakable joy. I spent hours upon hours blowing bubbles with my other children as we awaited her arrival. Unfortunately, her heart stopped beating around thirty-three weeks, and we delivered her on June 26, 2020. (You can read more about her story in the stillbirth section of this book.)

We had one final frozen embryo from our last IVF cycle. There was no way I could discard the embryo. After about six months, we decided to transfer our final embryo. We went in for our first ultrasound, and the doctor thought she saw two sacs. Her supervisor confirmed there were two. At that time, there were no visible heartbeats. The doctor warned us that she thought this would be a singleton pregnancy. Well, obviously, she did not know the God that we served. I have heard people say that God will give you double for your trouble. She didn't know all that we had been through up until this point.

My husband and I left that appointment believing we were pregnant with twins. We reminded ourselves of the multiple prophecies we received about having twins.

When we returned to the doctor the following week, we were ecstatic to see two flutters on the screen. Additional testing confirmed we were carrying identical twin boys. My blood pressure during this pregnancy was all over the place. Some days it was high, and other days it was low. When it was low, I did not feel well at all. I was light-headed, nauseated, and fatigued. I could not get myself together.

I went in for my routine doctor's visit and made the mistake of mentioning I had a cough I could not get rid of. I was immediately requested to go down to the emergency room for COVID testing. I asked the doctor if he could check the babies before I left, and he said no. Someone in labor and delivery would complete my visit after the results were back from testing. About five hours later, I was finally examined after my negative test result came back.

The first doctor had difficulty finding the babies. This was not uncommon. My boys loved playing hide-and-seek. With my help, she was able to locate them. She excused herself and said she would be right back. She returned with the midwife, who took over the examination. The midwife informed me that there was only one heartbeat. One of my babies died. I could not believe we were going through this again. How could this be happening again? I was in a daze. Dumbfounded. Confused. Sad.

The doctor gave me two options. I could go home with my family and speak with a maternal fetal specialist in the morning, or I could stay overnight in the hospital. She explained to me there was no special care that would be provided if I chose to remain in the hospital. At nineteen weeks, there would be no medical intervention if something were to happen to my remaining baby.

I decided to go home. My discharge papers did not mention the loss of one of the twins. My paperwork said I could return to activities as normal. What was normal about this? How was I supposed to return to life, to work like I had not just become aware that one of my babies was no longer with us? At the time, I was a child development teacher, and we were covering the prenatal unit. Many have said that I was strong, but I was not that strong and did not want to be. No one thought that I might need time to grieve the loss of my child? Furthermore, I did not know what to expect with regard to the loss of the baby. Would I have to deliver him? Would he remain in my womb until his brother was born? Would a dead baby in my womb cause health problems for the remaining twin?

I wrote a message to my obstetrician expressing my disappointment in the care I was receiving. She was on vacation. A social worker reached out to me. I had numerous questions, including why she was only calling because I complained about not being supported. Why didn't someone reach out automatically as soon as I experienced the loss of my child? She informed me that their office did not know one of the babies died. How was that possible? Why wouldn't labor and delivery inform my doctor that the baby died? Shouldn't the left hand be working with the right hand? Communication definitely needed to be improved. It should not be the patient's responsibility to inform the obstetrician of the loss when they all work for the same entity.

How could I remain joyful? How could I have a positive outlook? I had to make the choice to do so. I realized the need to shift my focus. Though I missed Tobias, Matthias was still with us. My other children were here and were in good health.

REFLECTION

God is the same yesterday, today, and forevermore. What He has done before, He can do again. What are you hoping God will do again?

* * *

Feel free to express your reflections creatively in the space below or on the following pages. Use words, images, colors, or any medium you prefer to document your thoughts and emotions. Let your creativity flow and capture your reflections in a way that feels authentic to you.

Sorry, Not Sorry

It took a while, but I have learned how to speak up and be an advocate for myself. This was not always the case. As a teenager and young adult, I often permitted others to run over me. I have since developed not only a voice for myself, but I have found myself advocating for children and the elders in our community who are often taken advantage of.

During my last pregnancy, Matthias liked playing hide-and-seek. Whenever an attempt was made to assess him via ultrasound, it was always difficult to find him. They had a hard time keeping him on the monitor. He was a very active baby.

My blood pressure was up and then down. Down and then up. I felt terrible. Early in the morning, I felt light-headed and faint. I could not shower, drive, or go to work. Mentally I was all over the place. I was grieving, angry, and fearful something was going to happen to Matthias. I ended up having an extended stay in the hospital so my medications could be titrated for my blood pressure. The team continually disagreed with whether I should be diagnosed with preeclampsia.

Almost every day, someone would make a comment about me wanting to get back home to my family. Though I missed my husband and our five children, I was not itching to go home. My greatest concern was coming home with a healthy baby boy and not coming home alone. I enjoyed being on the monitor hearing his heartbeat. It was reassurance that he was alive and well. There were a few nurses who would attempt to turn down the monitor, not considering the sound was a blessing and comfort to me.

My husband and I were able to find joy in our four weeks apart from one another. We realized this too was working together for our good. The odds of bringing home a healthy baby increased with the extra monitoring. I had to say sorry, not sorry. I will not apologize for fighting for my baby's life. Sorry, not sorry that the sound of his heartbeat is bothering you. Sorry, not sorry that we are still here.

REFLECTION

Identify a situation that surprisingly worked together for your good.

* * *

Feel free to express your reflections creatively in the space below or on the following pages. Use words, images, colors, or any medium you prefer to document your thoughts and emotions. Let your creativity flow and capture your reflections in a way that feels authentic to you.

It Is What It Is

" *When anxiety was great within me, your consolation brought me joy.*

— PSALM 94:19

L ife can be hard. Sometimes we find ourselves on a path that is unexpected. One thing I try to do is accept facts as they are. My faith does not refuse to face the facts. It is what it is.

That being the case, I had multiple concerns regarding the delivery of the twins. My previous C-sections resulted in major blood loss. The surgeons also had difficulty getting the babies out when delivering Malachi and Deja Joy. We were already grieving the loss of Tobias, and I did not want us to lose his twin, Matthias, as well. Therefore, I shared with my team my desire to be awake and to hold Tobias. I also told them about my history so they could be prepared with blood and patience.

After four weeks of being in the hospital for blood pressure issues, the doctors advised it was time to deliver the babies at thirty-two weeks. We had recently had a scare where they could not find a heartbeat for the baby. The whole staff was in my room ready to do whatever was necessary. Matthias's most recent ultrasound revealed that he was having issues with growth. My blood pressure was extremely high that night.

None of the medications were working in order to bring the pressure down. Once they got it under control, they put things in motion to deliver that morning.

The surgery was delayed because the surgery before mine was taking longer than expected. This delay worked together for my good. It provided time for my doctor to review my chart more closely. In doing so, she ordered blood products that were needed prior to surgery beginning.

As the surgery began, I could overhear the anesthesiologist being asked if he was going to attend a meeting. His response was he had the Zoom link, but he was not sure. In my mind, I was having a hard time understanding how he would be able to care for me and be attentive to a meeting at the same time. This created a lot of anxiety for me.

As the surgery moved forward, I had a hard time hearing what was going on in the other side of the drape. Chatty Kathy, another anesthesiologist, was running her mouth. She was loud and having personal conversations. My sacred moment with my baby was disrupted by unnecessary chatter. I lifted my head up off the table at one point and wanted to shout, "Shut up!" I found their disregard for me and my child disrespectful and unprofessional.

I sensed something was wrong. I told my husband something was wrong. When they took Matthias out of my womb, he was not crying. I had to inquire if he was okay. Someone eventually responded yes. His Apgar scores were 1 and 9. He was then rushed off to the NICU.

As the doctors continued to take care of me, there was great concern because of the large amount of blood I was losing. They could not discover the source. I lost 6.4 liters of blood. Once that was under control, they began to close my incisions. I could feel them closing me up. I asked the person closest to me if I should be feeling anything. I told her I was feeling it and that it hurt. She eventually said to them, "Hey, guys, she is feeling this. Did you titrate her epidural?" Still no relief.

I began to cry out in anguish, calling on the name of Jesus! I begged Him to help me. They finally came over and put a mask on my face and told me I was going to sleep now.

I woke up in the ICU intubated. I was confused, angry, and frustrated. I wanted to know about my baby. I needed to be able to talk. I begged them to take the tube out. The next day, I was able to return to labor and delivery. I wanted answers as to why I felt the closing of my incisions. No one gave me adequate answers.

My focus shifted to Matthias Justice, who weighed three pounds three ounces. Thanks be to God he was doing well. I was determined to get him home with our family by Christmas.

After my discharge, I went to spend time with Matthias every morning. My husband went to see him in the evening.

I noticed I was not the same woman after this delivery. I was angry. Hurt. Anxious. Depressed. Cautious. Overwhelmed. I felt helpless. I was not sleeping well. I often woke up biting my tongue and clenching my jaw. I thank God for my therapist, who I started seeing virtually after we lost Tobias at nineteen weeks. She helped me verbalize what was going on with me and make sense of it. Of course, I was not the same woman, and rightly so. I also began to see a psychiatrist and started taking Zoloft.

I had to tell myself it is what it is. Now what are you going to do? Yes, the pregnancy was rough. Yes, you lost one of your babies. Yes, the anesthesiologists messed up. Yes, you are still dealing with this trauma, and we do not know for how long. It is what it is. There are other things that are true also. God is a Healer. Holy Spirit is a comforter. Weeping may endure for a night, but joy comes in the morning. It is what it is.

REFLECTION

What contradictions have you faced that may get in the way of getting to joy?

* * *

Feel free to express your reflections creatively in the space below or on the following pages. Use words, images, colors, or any medium you prefer to document your thoughts and emotions. Let your creativity flow and capture your reflections in a way that feels authentic to you.

Final Thoughts

When I had my first thoughts about writing *Getting to JOY: A Mother's Journey of Infertility, Miscarriage, and Stillbirth*, I thought it was a book about conceiving and delivering a baby girl named Deja Joy. Silly me! Little did I know, it was so much more.

"For My thoughts *are* not your thoughts, nor *are* your ways My ways," says the Lord. "For *as* the heavens are higher than the earth, so are My ways higher than your ways, and My thoughts than your thoughts."

— ISAIAH 55:8–9

Little did I know about the journey. It led me to discover what real joy is and how it is possible to have joy despite less-than-desirable circumstances.

Please know that you are not on this journey by yourself. Please visit my website, tacolerobinson.com, or reach out to me on social media platforms. I am available to serve you through individual one-on-one ministry, book clubs, and other speaking engagements.

It is my hope that you have had some aha! moments while reading the scriptures, reading my experiences, and engaging in the reflections. It is my hope that you have found comfort in the prayers. It is my hope that you will choose JOY. Period.

 Now to Him who is able to do exceedingly abundantly above all that we ask or think, according to the power that works in us, to Him be glory in the church by Christ Jesus to all generations, forever and ever. Amen.

— EPHESIANS 3:20–21

Acknowledgments

I thank God for this work. He took my pain and disappointments and gave them purpose. I am honored to be entrusted with this ministry of healing. I do not serve alone.

I thank God for my husband, Marlon Robinson, who walks along the path with me. I appreciate your prayers, presence, and positive interactions with our children. I love you more than you realize.

I thank God for the medical professionals who hold a special place in my heart. Thank you for allowing God to use you that I may have the desires of my heart. Thank you to Dr. Jairo Garcia, Dr. Jeanne Sheffield, Mary LaHood, Nicole Davis, Dr. Ginny Merryman, Dr. Elena Ghiaur, Dr. Yangshu Pan, Dr. Camilla Yu, Dr. Emily S. Johnson, Dr. Jensara Clay, Dr. Chantel Cross, Dr. Teresa Fuller, and Susan Diaz.

I thank God for the aunties who have encouraged, prayed, and provided whatever our family may have needed over the years. Won't He do it!

I thank God for Butterfly Poet, aka my sister, Dikesha Robinson. Thank you for putting into words what our hearts felt and for allowing me to share your poem in this book.

I thank God for Ma, Marica Haire-Ellis. Thank you for proofreading, listening, encouraging, and loving me.

I thank God for my sissy, Michelle Johnson, and best friend, Ksha Lockett. God knows! You have seen me at my worst and at my best. You have never left my side. Your unconditional love showed up as prayers, presence, words of encouragement, tears, medical advice, listening ears, and a safe place to be me no matter where I found myself in the moment.

I thank God for His Holy Spirit. He showed me help would come from people I had not met yet. This assignment and ministry were new to me. There were so many uncertainties with moving forward. This was new territory.

I thank God for Nicole Queen. Your *yes* made all the difference in bringing this dream to fruition!

I thank God for Treya Cook. I appreciate you for sharing your creativity, time, wisdom, and words of prophecy.

About the Author

Elder Tacole Robinson is called to be a mother. There have been many challenges along the way, from infertility to fetal loss. Despite life's circumstances, she has found joy in the presence of a faithful God.

In 2005, she married her husband, Prophet Marlon Robinson. They have five sons and two daughters. As a foster parent, she has learned how to 'love and let go' of medically fragile children who need nurturance, healing, and stability. Together, they have a healing and deliverance ministry through Garden of Glory Ministries.

Elder Robinson desires to study to show herself approved by God; therefore, she is a lifelong learner. She has a Master of Divinity degree from Northern Baptist Theological Seminary and a Master of Education degree from The Ohio State University.

To gain insight into Tacole's journey toward motherhood, grab a copy of her book— *Getting to JOY: A Mother's Journey With Infertility, Miscarriage, and Stillbirth*. She bravely recounts her experiences with infertility, miscarriage, and stillbirth, which unexpectedly led her to find joy. Throughout the pages of this book, her heartfelt intention is to offer support, instill hope, and facilitate healing for individuals who are going through the process of grief.

You can connect with Tacole through her personal ministry, *Tacole Robinson Ministries*, which can be found on all social media platforms and her website: www.tacolerobinson.com.

www.ingramcontent.com/pod-product-compliance
Lightning Source LLC
Chambersburg PA
CBHW051523120626

46551CB00012B/1059